STARS in the SPOTLIGHT

Keira Knightley

Colleen Adams

press™

New York

Published in 2007 by The Rosen Publishing Group, Inc.
29 East 21st Street, New York, NY 10010

Book Design: Haley WIlson

Photo Credits: Cover, p. 4 © Robyn Beck/AFP/Getty Images; pp. 6, 16 © Vince Bucci/Getty Images; p. 8 © Kevin Winter/Getty Images; pp. 10, 14, 24 © Evan Agostini/Getty Images; p. 12 © AFP/AFP/Getty Images; p. 18 © Mark Mainz/Getty Images; p. 20 © ShowBizreland.com/Getty Images; pp. 22, 26 © Dave Hogan/Getty Images; p. 28 © Frazer Harrison/Getty Images.

Library of Congress Cataloging-in-Publication Data

Adams, Colleen.
  Keira Knightley / Colleen Adams.
     p. cm. - (Stars in the spotlight)
  Includes index.
  ISBN-13: 978-1-4042-3513-2
  ISBN-10: 1-4042-3513-2 (library binding)
 1. Knightley, Keira, 1985-Juvenile literature. 2. Motion picture actors and actresses-Great Britain-Biography-Juvenile literature. I. Title. II. Series.
  PN2598.K74A33 2006
  791.4302'8092-dc22
  [B]
                              2006014621

Manufactured in the United States of America

Contents

A Famous Actress

Keira Knightley is a popular British actress. She has been working since she was 7 years old. Her first role was on a television show. Her first role in a popular movie came in 1999. She was **cast** in a small part in *Star Wars: Episode I–The Phantom Menace*. Keira continued working through her teen years. Movies like *Bend It Like Beckham* in 2002 and *Pirates of the Caribbean: The Curse of the Black Pearl* in 2003 have made her a well-known actress. Her performance in the movie *Pride and Prejudice* earned her award **nominations** for best actress in 2006.

Keira is shown here at the 2006 Academy Awards ceremony at the Kodak Theatre in Hollywood, California.

An Early Start

Keira's parents and older brother, Caleb, welcomed her into the world on March 26, 1985. She grew up in Richmond, near London, England. Keira's dad, Will Knightley, worked as an actor in the theater and on television. Keira's mom, Sharman Macdonald, worked as an actress and a **playwright**.

When she was 3 years old, Keira saw her mom and dad getting calls from **agents**. She decided she wanted an agent, too! Her parents finally agreed to get her an agent when she was 6. They told her she could only work during summer breaks. In 1993, Keira got her first small role in a television show called *Royal Celebration*.

Keira is shown here with her father (far left), mother, and older brother, Caleb (far right), celebrating at a party before the 2006 Academy Awards.

7

A Struggle with Reading

Keira attended Teddington School near her home. School was not always fun for her because she struggled with reading. Keira has a learning disability called **dyslexia**. She often reads words and numbers backwards. Keira's classmates made fun of her because she couldn't read well. She often **memorized** tapes of her schoolbooks to keep other students from making fun of her. Keira's mother always insisted that her daughter's education come first. She told Keira that she had to continue reading and studying during the summer if she wanted to keep acting.

Keira is shown here with her mom, Sharman Macdonald, at a party after the Golden Globe Awards in January 2006.

A Child Actress

When Keira was 9, she was cast as Natasha Jordan in a movie called *A Village Affair*. After that, she played small roles in several British television shows. When she was 11, Keira was cast as a princess in *Treasure Seekers*. In 1998, she was chosen to play the character of Judith Dunbar as a young girl in the television show *Coming Home*. It was a story that followed the lives of two girls growing up in the 1930s and 1940s. As a teenager, Keira took acting classes at a local youth club but never went to acting school.

Keira knew at a young age that she wanted to be an actress. Small parts on television shows and in movies helped her get starring roles as a teenager. Here she signs autographs for fans at the opening of *Pride and Prejudice* in 2005.

The Big Break or Not?

Keira was offered the part of Sabé in the movie *Star Wars: Episode I–The Phantom Menace*. She was chosen because she looked so much like Natalie Portman, who played Queen Amidala. In the movie, Sabé is dressed to look like the queen and is used as a **decoy**. Many people did not know that Keira appeared in this movie because director George Lucas kept it a secret. He wanted people to think that Portman played both roles. For this reason, Keira did not receive a lot of attention for acting in this popular movie. Some people still think that Portman played both parts.

Shown here are Natalie Portman and Hayden Christensen in *Star Wars: Episode II–The Phantom Menace*. Even devoted Star War fans could not tell that the roles of Sabé and Queen Amidala were played by two different actresses.

Princess of Thieves

In 2001, Keira was chosen to star in a television movie called *Princess of Thieves*. She played the part of Gwyn, the daughter of Robin Hood and Maid Marion. In the movie, King Richard of England is dying. His son Philip must travel from France to England to stop Prince John, Richard's brother, from taking over the throne. Richard orders Robin Hood and Will Scarlett to bring Philip safely back to England, but they are captured. Against her father's wishes, Gwyn and Philip set out to free Robin and Will. The four of them then go on to save Philip's throne. This was Keira's first starring role on a television show.

As Gwyn in *Princess of Thieves*, Keira had to learn to shoot arrows and ride a horse. She would later go on to play many other action roles in movies.

15

Bend It Like Beckham

In 2002, Keira was cast in the role of Juliette "Jules" Paxton in the movie *Bend It Like Beckham*. The story is about Jess Bhamra, an 18-year-old girl who lives in London with her traditional Indian family. Jess dreams of playing soccer like her hero, soccer star David Beckham. However, her parents will not allow her to play. When she meets Jules, she gets a chance to play on a women's soccer team. Jess plays on the team but keeps it a secret from her parents. As best friends, Jess and Jules deal with the challenges of playing soccer and growing up. This movie was a big hit first in England, then in the United States.

Keira is shown at a party in Hollywood, California, with actress Parminder Nagra, who played Jess in *Bend It Like Beckham*.

Balancing School and Acting

Keira had a busy schedule that included hours of soccer training for her role in *Bend It Like Beckham*. She also had to keep up with her schoolwork at Teddington School. In the summer of 2001, Keira took her final exams and passed with all A's. She went on to take courses in art, history, and English at Esher College for a short time. Keira still struggles with dyslexia. She said, "I can learn scripts fine. It's just the reading of them in the first place that is a problem." In 2003, she was chosen to represent the British Dyslexia Association. She has also helped out with other **charity** events.

Keira is shown at a charity event in Hollywood in February 2006.

Pirates of the Caribbean

After the success of *Bend It Like Beckham*, Keira was offered several other starring roles in movies. In 2003, she was cast in *Pirates of the Caribbean: The Curse of the Black Pearl*, which also starred actors Orlando Bloom and Johnny Depp. In the movie, Keira plays Elizabeth Swann, who is captured by the evil pirate Captain Barbossa. Will Turner, Elizabeth's childhood friend, and Captain Jack Sparrow team up to save her. In their adventure, they discover the truth behind the curse of the *Black Pearl* pirate ship and find a lost treasure.

Keira is shown standing in front of a poster for *Pirates of the Caribbean: The Curse of the Black Pearl* at the movie's opening. The poster shows Captain Jack Sparrow, played by Johnny Depp.

KIN
RTH
22
THE UNTOLD TRUE STORY THAT

King Arthur

In 2003, Keira traveled to Ireland and Wales to play the part of Guinevere in the movie *King Arthur*. In this **version** of the **legend** of King Arthur, Arthur is a Roman general during the time of the fall of the Roman Empire. After 15 years of fighting in Britain, Arthur and his knights are given one final mission before they return to Rome. This mission leads Arthur to realize that when the Roman army leaves Britain, the **invasion** of the Saxons will destroy the country. Guinevere helps Arthur understand that he must stay to lead Britain and change the course of history.

Keira is shown at the opening of the movie *King Arthur* in London, England.

23

Pride and Prejudice

The movie *Pride and Prejudice* was **adapted** from a book by famous author Jane Austen. Keira played the part of Elizabeth (Lizzie) Bennet. Elizabeth is the second oldest of five sisters who live in England near the end of the 1700s. Their mother wants each of her daughters to marry a wealthy gentleman. When Lizzie meets the rich and handsome Mr. Darcy, she thinks that he is rude and **snobbish**. However, a series of events changes Lizzie's **opinion**. She falls in love with Darcy and realizes he is the man she wants to marry.

Keira is shown here with Matthew Macfadyen, who played the role of Mr. Darcy in the movie *Pride and Prejudice.*

More Pirate Movies

Pirates of the Caribbean: The Curse of the Black Pearl was a big hit in 2003. Plans were made to make two more movies. In *Pirates of the Caribbean: Dead Man's Chest*, Captain Jack Sparrow, Will Turner, and Elizabeth Swann once again take part in another adventure. In this movie, Captain Jack Sparrow must settle a debt with the legendary Davey Jones, captain of the ghost ship the *Flying Dutchman*. Jack must save himself or be forced to serve Davey Jones in the **afterlife**. Will and Elizabeth delay their wedding to help Jack.

Keira once again played the role of Elizabeth Swann in *Pirates of the Caribbean: Dead Man's Chest*. This movie appeared in theaters in the summer of 2006.

27

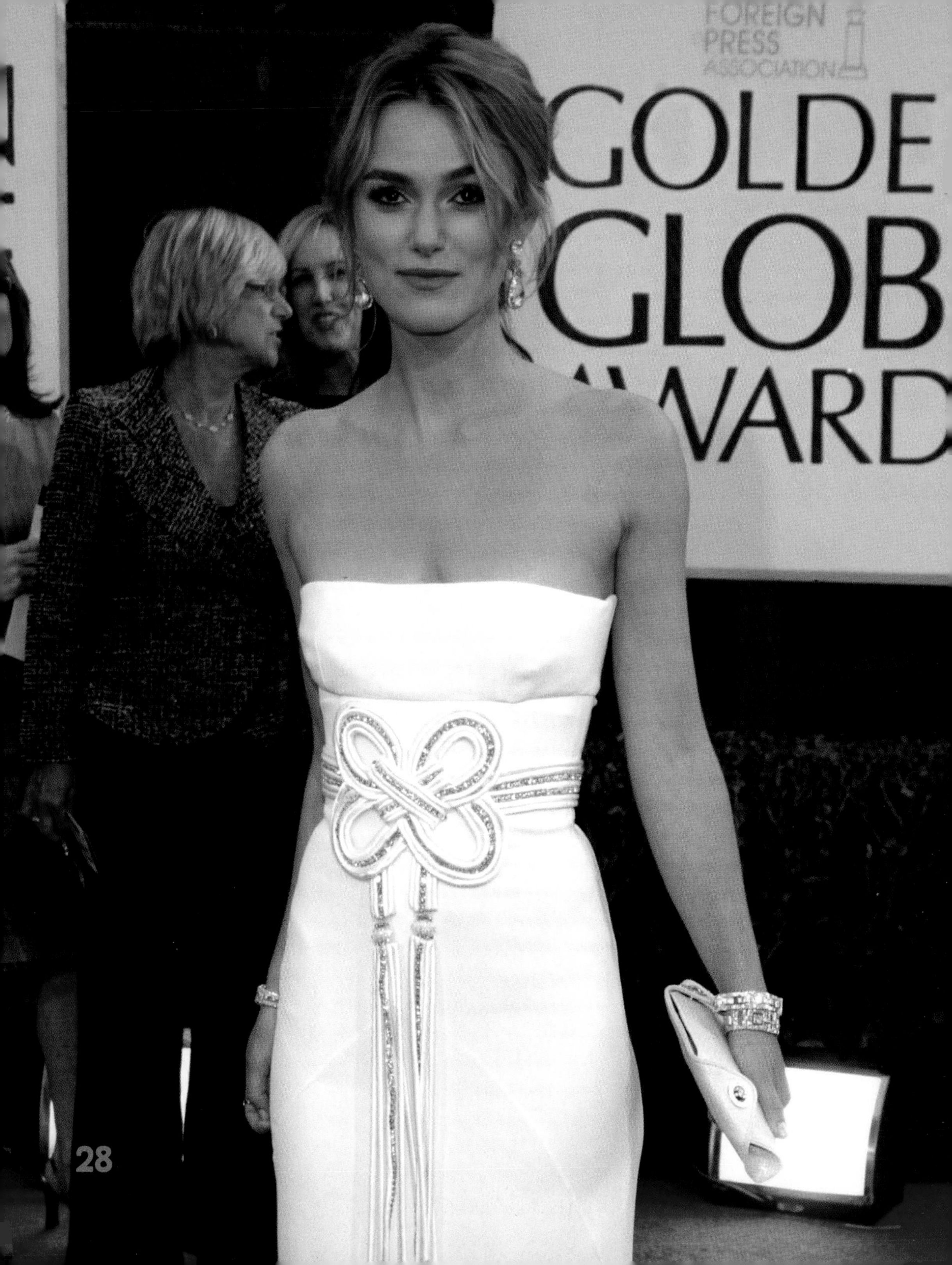
FOREIGN
PRESS
ASSOCIATION
GOLDE
GLOB
AWARD

Action Roles

Keira is often in movies that have many action scenes. She will also appear in a third *Pirates of the Caribbean* movie with costars Johnny Depp and Orlando Bloom in 2007. Keira has said she likes the challenge of learning new skills for the roles she plays. She trained as a soccer player when she played Jules in *Bend It Like Beckham*. As Elizabeth in *Pirates of the Caribbean: Curse of the Black Pearl*, she had to walk off the end of a moving plank. To play Guinevere in *King Arthur*, Keira learned **archery** and sword fighting. Knightley has shown that she is a talented actress who is not afraid to try new things.

Keira received a Golden Globe and an Academy Award nomination for Best Actress for her role as Elizabeth Bennet in *Pride and Prejudice.* She is shown here at the Golden Globe Awards in 2006.

29

Keira's Success

Keira Knightley is one of today's most successful young actresses. Her ability to portray strong young women has made her popular with movie fans. Keira's performance as Elizabeth Bennet in the movie *Pride and Prejudice* earned her both a Golden Globe and an Academy Award nomination for Best Actress. She is now able to choose from many offers for acting roles. Though she began as a child actress struggling with dyslexia, she has overcome many challenges. Keira Knightley has come a long way to reach her dream.

Glossary

adapt (uh-DAPT) To change something so that it will work well for a new purpose.

afterlife (AF-tuhr-lyf) Existence after death.

agent (AY-juhnt) A person who acts or does business for another.

archery (AHR-chuh-ree) The sport or practice of using a bow and arrows.

cast (KAST) To assign a part or a role to.

charity (CHAIR-uh-tee) Help given to people in need.

decoy (DEE-koy) A person or a thing that is used to draw attention away from someone or something else.

dyslexia (dihs-LEHK-see-uh) A learning disability that involves problems with reading, writing, and spelling. A person with dyslexia may see and write letters and numbers backwards.

invasion (in-VAY-zhun) The act of entering by force to conquer.

legend (LEH-juhnd) An old story that is widely believed but cannot be proven to be true.

memorize (MEH-muh-ryz) To learn something by heart.

nomination (nah-muh-NAY-shun) The act of choosing someone as a candidate for a certain honor.

opinion (uh-PIHN-yuhn) A belief based on experience and certain facts.

playwright (PLAY-ryt) A person who writes plays.

snobbish (SNAH-bish) Wanting to be with people of higher social position and looking down on or avoiding those felt to be less important.

version (VUHR-zhun) An account or description from a certain point of view.

Index

Web Sites

Due to the changing nature of Internet links, PowerKids Press has develo
an online list of Web sites related to the subject of this book. This site is
updated regularly. Please use this link to access the list:
http://www.powerkidslinks.com/stars/knightley/